FROM SHACKLES TO FREEDOM

A Born-Again Story

MARITZA PEREZ

This book is a work of non-fiction based on the author's personal experiences. Names, places, and identifying details have been changed where appropriate to protect privacy.

Published by
IWFN Publishing

(It Wasn't for Nothing Publishing LLC)

ISBN (Paperback): 978-1-969886-04-1
ISBN (Hardcover): 978-1-969886-05-8

Printed in the United States of America.

Contents

Dedication...5

Author's Note..7

Acknowledgements 9

CHAPTER ONE: THE ACHE TO BELONG 12

CHAPTER TWO: SENT AWAY 18

CHAPTER THREE: LOOKING FOR GOD IN
ALL THE WRONG PLACES 24

CHAPTER FOUR: WHEN GOD CAME FOR ME 34

CHAPTER FIVE: WHEN FREEDOM STARTED
TO FEEL FAMILIAR, AND FEAR RETURNED 40

CHAPTER SIX: UNLEARNING FEAR
TO RECLAIM FAITH 48

CHAPTER SEVEN: FEARLESS FAITH:
LEAVING WITHOUT LEAVING GOD 54

CHAPTER EIGHT: THE LIES THAT FELL AWAY..................60

CHAPTER NINE: BECOMING WITHOUT APOLOGY 64

CHAPTER TEN: THE CHURCH JESUS IMAGINED 70

CHAPTER ELEVEN: FAITH WITHOUT FEAR.....................74

CHAPTER TWELVE: COMMUNITY
WITHOUT CONDITIONS..78

CHAPTER THIRTEEN: THE NARROW ROAD
OF FREEDOM...82

CHAPTER FOURTEEN: THE WORD AND
THE LIVING GOD 86

CHAPTER FIFTEEN: FREEDOM
REQUIRES DISCERNMENT 90

CHAPTER SIXTEEN: THE STRENGTH
OF BOUNDARIES 94

CHAPTER SEVENTEEN: ALONENESS IS
NOT LONELINESS..98

CHAPTER EIGHTEEN: WHEN REJECTION
NO LONGER DEFINES YOU 104

CHAPTER NINETEEN: GUARDING
THE HEART WITHOUT BUILDING WALLS.......................110

CHAPTER TWENTY: BECOMING SAFE TO YOURSELF 114

FINAL CHAPTER: FROM SHACKLES TO FREEDOM...........120

A Closing Reflection 125

Dedication

For those who learned to survive before they learned to feel safe.

For the ones who were taught to earn love instead of receiving it.

For those who carried faith in their hands while fear quietly settled in their bones.

For the ones who stayed too long, tried too hard, and believed their worth depended on being chosen.

For those who questioned what they were taught yet still longed for God with an honest heart.

This book is for the ones who walked away not because they stopped believing, but because they refused to stop becoming.

For those who have felt unseen in sacred spaces, misunderstood in moments of courage, and judged for choosing healing over performance.

May these pages remind you that your story matters. That your questions are holy. That your longing is not rebellion—it is remembrance.

And that freedom has always been part of your inheritance.

Author's Note

This book was not written to persuade, convince, or dismantle anyone's beliefs. It was written to tell the truth — my truth — as faithfully and honestly as I know how.

What follows is not theology, doctrine, or instruction. It is a lived story. A testimony shaped by longing, faith, disillusionment, healing, and grace. It is not meant to represent all believers, all churches, or all spiritual experiences. It simply reflects mine.

I write as someone who loves God deeply and who has wrestled deeply with faith. I write as someone who has known both the beauty and the burden of religious spaces. I write as someone who has walked through devotion, fear, obedience, rebellion, and return — often all at once.

This book is not an argument against the church, nor is it a rejection of faith. It is an honest exploration of what happens when faith becomes entangled with fear, when belonging becomes conditional, and when love is confused with performance. It is also a testimony of how grace can still find us there.

Some of what you read may resonate. Some may challenge you. Some may even discomfort you. That is okay. This book does not demand agreement — only presence. You are invited to read slowly, to pause when something stirs, and to notice what rises within you.

I believe truth is not threatened by questions. I believe faith grows stronger when it is examined with humility and compassion. And I believe that God is far more patient, loving, and expansive than many of us were taught.

If you find yourself reflected in these pages, know that you are not alone. If you find yourself disagreeing, I honor your journey as well. This is not about right or wrong — it is about honesty.

Above all, this book is an offering of hope:

that healing is possible,

that freedom is not rebellion,

and that love does not withdraw when we begin to ask deeper questions.

May these words meet you gently.

May they invite reflection, not fear.

And may you feel free to breathe as you read.

Acknowledgements

This book exists because of the many people—seen and unseen—who crossed my path and shaped my becoming.

First and foremost, I thank God. Not the version I was taught to fear, but the One who met me in my unraveling and stayed. The One who never demanded perfection, only honesty. The One who carried me when I could no longer carry myself.

I acknowledge the people who walked with me during seasons of confusion, loss, and rebuilding—those who listened without trying to fix me, who offered presence instead of answers. Some of you may not even know the impact you had, but your kindness became a lifeline when I needed it most.

I honor the teachers, mentors, and guides who helped me see beyond fear and performance, who reminded me that growth is not linear and faith is not fragile. Even those whose influence came through contrast or disappointment played a role in my awakening. Every encounter taught me something.

To my children—thank you for being my greatest teachers. You showed me what love looks like when it's honest, unfiltered, and brave. You taught me humility, resilience, and the courage to keep choosing growth even when it was uncomfortable.

To the friends who stayed when I questioned everything, and to those who gently stepped away—thank you. Each relationship revealed something true, even when it hurt.

And to the version of myself who kept going when it would have been easier to shut down: I see you now. I honor your endurance, your softness, and your willingness to begin again.

Finally, to the reader—thank you for trusting me with your time and your heart. If something in these pages resonated with you, know that you are not alone. Your story matters. Your questions matter. And your healing matters more than you know.

CHAPTER ONE:

THE ACHE TO BELONG

Feeling unwanted is not a thought—it is a condition of the soul.

For me, it lived in my body long before I could name it. A tightening in my chest. A constant alertness. A sense that I had to earn my place in the world or risk disappearing altogether.

My father was absent—not just physically, but emotionally. The only time I saw my father was during summer breaks. But even then, I felt as if I were a burden.

My mother was consumed by survival. She moved from one relationship to another, always needing a man, always believing that love—however unstable—was better than being alone. I watched her choose men who harmed her, and by extension, harmed me. She married toxicity again and again, and I learned early that love was something you endured, not something that protected you.

I don't believe she meant to hurt me. I believe she was wounded herself. In hindsight, I recognize she was desperately seeking love but didn't know what that looked like. But as a child, all I knew was that I came second to the men in her life.

And when she wasn't there, others were.

They crossed lines that should never have been crossed.

I didn't have language for sexual abuse. I only knew that something inside me broke and that speaking up felt dangerous. I learned silence. I learned to leave my body while staying present. I learned how to survive.

What hurt almost as much as the abuse itself was the sense that my mother knew something was wrong and did nothing. Whether out of denial, fear, or survival, her inaction told me something devastating: my safety was not worth disrupting her world. A world that gave her a false sense of love and security.

That belief became a blueprint for my life.

I learned to accept crumbs and call it love. I learned to confuse attention with affection. I learned that love meant tolerating pain.

As I grew older, that belief took shape in rebellion. I wasn't trying to be reckless—I was trying to reclaim control. If I could choose who wanted me, then maybe I could rewrite the story where I once had no choice.

But what I called empowerment was actually survival in disguise.

I sought closeness through sex, mistaking desire for worth. I told myself I was free, but inside I was still that little girl trying to be chosen. I became pregnant—twice—and each time, fear swallowed me whole. I was still a child myself, carrying adult decisions I had no framework to hold.

I had two abortions before I ever left high school.

Neither were my choices. They were acts of desperation. The first one was my mother's attempt to solve a crisis. I was only 14 years old. A baby would be too much for her. The second one I was seventeen, I had a severe case of chicken pox during my first trimester. The doctor highly recommended I abort because the chances of holding a healthy baby in my arms were vanishingly small. I felt I had no choice. To make matters worse, my boyfriend dumped me soon after. I felt ashamed and utterly alone. I didn't grieve because I didn't know how. I buried the pain and told myself to move on.

But loss has a way of waiting.

I dropped out of high school carrying more weight than any teenager should. I felt defective. Behind. Ashamed. I told myself I had ruined my life before it even started. I got pregnant for a third time. This time I was keeping my baby. I did. Then I got pregnant again. By the age of 20 I had 2 kids. I was grateful my boyfriend, who later became my husband, stuck it out with me. I wasn't physically alone, but inside I was in despair. How did I end up like this?

And yet, somewhere deep inside, there was a flicker of defiance.

I refused to become the life I came from.

I refused to repeat my mother's story—even as I unknowingly followed its emotional patterns.

I told myself I would do better. I would not depend on anyone. I would not be weak. I would not be abandoned.

So, I became relentless. I got my GED. I went to college. I studied while exhausted and overwhelmed.

I pushed through sleepless nights and relentless pressure because I believed success would save me. That stability would heal what love had broken. Eventually, I became a pharmacist.

From the outside, it looked like triumph. I had escaped. I had succeeded. I had rewritten the narrative.

But inside, I was still running. I had traded chaos for control, not for peace. I gave my children a better life materially, but I was often emotionally absent—exhausted from carrying the weight of proving I was better than where I came from. I told myself I was nothing like my mother. But I was repeating parts of her story in another form. She sought safety through men. I sought safety through achievement. Both of us were trying to outrun pain. I worked myself into the ground. I built a life that looked stable from the outside while inside I remained fractured. I believed worth had to be earned. I believed rest was dangerous. I believed love had conditions. And yet, even in the middle of all that striving, something in me ached for more—not more success, not more validation—but something I couldn't name.

I didn't yet know it was God.

I only knew I was tired of surviving.

And that question—Is this really what love is supposed to feel like? —would eventually crack everything open.

CHAPTER TWO:

SENT AWAY

I was sent away after my first abortion.

In my mother's mind, she was mourning the loss of a control she never actually possessed, grieving a ghost of authority. Bottom line: I had become inconvenient.

My mother decided I would go live with my father—someone who had never truly been a presence in my life except during a couple of summer breaks when I'd visit. But sexual abused followed me even there. It was as if I had a sign on me that said have your way with me. I was repeatedly abused by my stepsister. This is a secret so heavy I have protected until now. Abuse from an adult is destructive to mind, body, and soul. But abuse from someone of my same sex and age, that is another level of perniciousness that is inexplicable.

Sending me away was not framed as abandonment, but that is what it felt like. I remember the moment clearly: the quiet finality of it. No conversation about how I felt. No reassurance that I mattered. Just the unspoken message that I was a problem to be managed.

My father lived in another state, in a world I did not belong to. In my eyes he was living the American dream. A white picket fenced house in the suburbs, a wife, and perfect kids. Although I was his daughter, I entered their home as an outsider, already labeled before I even spoke. The problem child.

I learned quickly that affection there was conditional.

My father was strict, emotionally distant, and deeply critical. His love came with expectations I could never fully meet. I was not allowed to be a child. I was not allowed to make mistakes. I certainly was not allowed to need.

When I disappointed him, he did not correct me, he rejected me. That rejection carved something deep inside me. I learned that love could be withdrawn at any moment. I learned to measure my worth by behavior, performance, obedience.

And yet, even in that rigid environment, I was still a child carrying unresolved trauma. I had already been abused. I was already confused about my body, my value, my role in the world. No one saw that. No one asked. Instead, I was expected to fall in line. The worse part was that my father would compare me to my stepsister. She was perfect and I was not. That is how that translated to me. He was clueless to the darkness she carried.

When I began to develop physically, the attention I received only deepened the confusion. I did not understand the power my body seemed to hold, only that it got reactions. Attention felt like validation. Validation felt like safety. But it was also a source of power I used on my stepsister. She could no longer touch me without my consent. It was my first time setting a boundary.

That is when I began to equate being wanted with being worthy. It gave me a false sense of control.

I choose who could love me. That is what I thought. The irony is that I desperately wanted to be chosen by the very people who couldn't love me safely. I wanted my father's approval. I wanted my mother's protection. I wanted someone to see me and say, you matter. Instead, I learned to perform. I learned to shape myself into what others expected, quiet when necessary, pleasing when useful, invisible when inconvenient. I learned that being liked was safer than being known.

When I eventually dropped out of high school, it was not rebellion, it was resignation. I already believed I had failed. I already believed I was behind. I told myself I would figure it out later, but deep down I felt like I was confirming what everyone else already thought about me. I carried shame like a second skin. Yet even then, something in me refused to disappear.

I got my GED not because I believed in myself, but because I did not want my story to end there. I had already experienced too much loss to let my life collapse entirely. I pushed forward not with confidence, but with desperation. I became a mother while still trying to figure out how to be a child. I loved my children fiercely, but love did not erase my wounds. I was still learning how to survive while trying to raise kids. I wanted to give them stability, safety, a life better than mine. To me, that meant love. I told myself that if I could just work harder, provide more, and stay strong, everything would be okay.

So, I worked. And worked. And worked.

I pursued education. I pursued security. I pursued control. I built a life that looked stable from the outside but felt hollow inside. I replaced emotional connection with productivity. I mistook exhaustion for purpose. And yet, even as I achieved more, I felt less at home in myself. The truth was, I did not know how to rest. I did not know how to receive care without suspicion. I did not know how to be loved without earning it.

I had learned too young that love was conditional, and I carried that lesson everywhere. By the time I reached adulthood, I wasn't just surviving trauma anymore. I was living inside its architecture.

And still, somewhere beneath the striving and the fear, there was a quiet ache, an unanswered question that refused to die: Is this really what love is supposed to feel like?

CHAPTER THREE:

LOOKING FOR GOD IN ALL THE WRONG PLACES

I didn't marry because I was in love. I married because I was afraid of what my life would look like if I did not. I asked him to marry me. There was no proposal, no celebration, just a courthouse and a trip to the DMV to change my last name. I wanted legitimacy. I wanted the same last name as my children. I wanted proof that I had not failed.

Marriage gave me relief, not joy.

We were young, wounded, and unprepared. Finances were chaotic. Arguments were constant. We both came from broken homes and carried unresolved trauma into our relationship. Neither of us knew what love looked like. He cheated. Or at least, I knew something was wrong even when he denied it. Anxiety turned into rage. The relationship became toxic.

And yet, I stayed.

Motherhood and marriage motivated me to build a future. I believed financial security would save us. If we could just escape poverty, everything else would fall into place.

So I worked relentlessly.

I earned my degree. Became a pharmacist. Bought a home. Moved to Florida. From the outside, it looked like success. Inside, I was lonelier than ever. I worked long hours, sometimes fourteen, sometimes more. I cooked before work and cleaned after. The house got bigger, the workload heavier. I carried the financial weight of the family yet felt invisible.

In the community, I wasn't known by my name. I was known as his wife, the pharmacist. I had status. But no sense of self. He accused me constantly of cheating, projecting what he himself was doing. Until one day, the accusation became truth. I crossed a line I swore I never would.

When the confrontation turned physical, something inside me broke. I did not leave for another man. I left because I hated who I had become. I could not live with myself.

I left out of guilt, not freedom.

And in the aftermath, a deeper hunger surfaced:

Who am I?

Why am I on repeat?

What am I missing?

That question opened a door I did not know how to close.

Growing up, I had watched my mother seek answers through spiritual readings. So, when I found myself desperate for meaning, Santeria felt familiar, mystical, ancient, personal. It spoke to pain. It promised insight. It offered belonging.

My first reading shook me. I shared nothing, yet the man described my past, my trauma, my infidelity with unsettling accuracy. I broke down. For the first time in a long time, I felt seen. I mistook recognition for healing. I returned repeatedly, paying for rituals, cleansing, protection. I wanted answers. I wanted safety. I wanted someone to tell me I was not broken. Yet I yearned for physical touch. It was what I equated with love.

I ended up returning to the man I had cheated with. Although I had left my marriage, he stayed in his. He stayed out of fear of losing his kids. Our affair was known by everyone including his wife. I was addicted to the wreckage, finding solace in his flaws that mirrored my own. This shared brokenness forged a bond that felt like home, even as it systematically dismantled me, piece by painful piece. I endured a year and a half of being his second choice before I finally found the strength to walk away. At the time, I thought I was simply ending a cycle of neglect; I had no way of knowing that my goodbye would become a permanent silence, the final words we would ever exchange.

He was killed in a head on collision that same night I broke things off. Every fear I had suddenly became my nightmare. I had dreamt something bad was going to happen. It was a prophecy I shared with him: if he were to die I would be banned from his funeral. He laughed at the thought declaring himself healthy as an ox. He said it would not happen, right up until the moment my worse fear ripped reality apart. His mother blamed me. His wife banned me from attending the funeral. Grief turned into guilt, and guilt drove me deeper into the religion.

I fully committed. I was baptized into Santeria. This was not for the faint of heart. Not only does it require dedication, it was extremely expensive. It was a ritual that lasted a week, then a year long of adhering to strict rules under the guidance of a padrino (spiritual leader). Baptism symbolized the death of the old self and the rebirth of new self. It was ritualized by having me enter a lake fully clothed with the the shabbiest clothes I had. Once in the lake, priestess would tear off my clothes. I emerged from the water completely naked. The priestess would then dress me in brand new white garments. My head was shaved off. I had to wear never worn white clothes for an entire year. No fragrances or make-up. Anything I put on my skin had to be natural. Coconut was what I was instructed to use. I followed every rule.

This is Santeria's version of being born again.

What I did not recognize was the manipulation. The control. The cost. I would stay in this religion for seven years. For a long time, I felt as if I belonged, my padrino took me everywhere. I was his apprentice. In hindsight, I was more like his golden goose. I covered all his expenses. My desire to belong, be loved, blinded me to the manipulation.

Until one day he crossed boundaries while intoxicated. Panic froze me. The knots in my gut clenched me and my chest tightened in fear. A familiar feeling but I ignored the alarm inside me because obedience felt safer than questioning.

When he told me to sell my house and give him the proceeds for a "business," I complied.

Belonging blinded me.

The business turned out to be illegal. I lived next door to it in shame and fear. Eventually, I made an anonymous call and reported it to the police.

When he discovered I had left, with help from my ex-husband, he cursed me and told me I would regret it for the rest of my life.

I believed him. I moved back to New Jersey to escape it all.

Santeria provided me a sense of guidance. Without the readings I felt lost. Terrified I sought another padrino to give me a reading. I was able to go to one with the help of my mother. I eagerly went to meet him for answers, but when I met him, I felt a great sense of uneasiness. He was not what I was used to.

He was different. He seemed possessed.

He began his chants in Spanish, then some other language I did not understand. But then a voice came out of him—clear, sharp, unmistakably not his own, asking me:

"What are you looking for here?

This is a religion of the poor.

You do not belong here."

I froze.

My body knew something was wrong, but my heart was too afraid to leave. Leaving meant being alone again. And loneliness had always felt more dangerous than bondage. I did not go back. I continued doing rituals on my own such as the cigar and liquor rituals I was taught. That was all I knew how to do. I never learned how to do readings. Although baptism made me a priestess, I was a handicapped one. Unable to sustain myself. I was lost.

It would be a couple of years before I got entangled in a relationship that would mark the beginning of an end. The red flags were there...anger, functioning alcoholic, no family, or friends he ever presented to me. But I ignored the signs. After all, he told me he loved me. When he held me, I felt loved. I did not know how to discern if it was genuine.

One day, I heard him call my daughter a f*^king whore. Had he called me that, I would not have flinched. It would've hurt but not enough to remain alone. But when he said it to my daughter, I lashed out in anger. I did what I wanted my mom to do to my stepdad. I threw him out. I would never choose a man over my children. This happened the day he was moving in with me. I put an end to it. I wish I could say we parted peacefully, But that would be pure wishful thinking. His anger would not let him just go away. He was determined to seek vengeance for throwing him out.

He accused me of prescription fraud. It would take several months but he managed to get me arrested. During the time we dated, I did sell him a prescription for eye drops used for pink eye without a valid prescription. It was a gesture of compassion but in the eyes of law it was fraud. I also got charged for insurance fraud since I billed his insurance. Anyone reading the charges would think I was profiting millions in fraudulent prescription sales. It was a $7 eye drop that cost me significantly more...

My career, everything I had worked for, disappeared overnight.

From six figures to nothing.

I lost my job. My security. My identity.

Fortunately, I had a friend who came to my rescue. I moved back to Florida where my friend gave me work. My pharmacist license was flagged; no corporate pharmacy would hire me. Once in Florida, I sought a padrino again. I was tired of being lost. I wanted answers. Why was this happening to me?

I met one who seemed great. He was a family person. Spiritual leader was not his full-time job; it was something he practiced through faith. I felt comfortable under his wings. Until I got a reading from him that would be my last one. It wasn't just the familiar knot in my gut and the tightness in my chest, it was as if my heart was yanked out of my chest, chopped up and given back to me to chew. He told me that I had to take part in a ritual to rid me of this "curse" that was keeping me in bondage. Only a seed of a priest could rid my curse. Sex was the answer. Since he was a priest, he qualified for the ritual. I knew this man's wife! How could he stand there and tell me this as if it was no big deal?!!

Anger and rage consumed me. I cursed out God. I hated Him.

Why did You make me to just be abused??!! Just kill me already!! Take me out of my misery! That was my cry to the heavens. I drove home crying uncontrollably, barely able to keep my eyes open. When I got home, I threw everything away, every artifact, every idol, every symbol.

I was done.

Not just with the religion, but with God. I did not know yet that collapse was not the end. But it was the moment I stopped running.

CHAPTER FOUR:

WHEN GOD CAME FOR ME

After I walked away from Santeria and told God to take my life, I lived with a quiet but constant anxiety. He was going to wipe me off this earth. I felt like a failure in every sense, spiritually, relationally, professionally. I had nothing left to offer. And I did not see the point in moving forward.

I was waiting for judgment.

I was waiting for punishment.

I was waiting for death.

Instead, God met me at a bar.

That is where I was first introduced to Christianity, not through a pulpit, not through a sermon, not through a church building. Through a man who simply listened to me. I said all kinds of wild, broken, chaotic things, and he did not flinch. He did not correct me. He did not judge me. There was something about him that I could not name at the time, but I wanted whatever he had.

Now I know what it was.

Peace.

He told me to read the Bible. And the next day, that is exactly what I did. I bought one and opened it to the New Testament. The Old Testament felt too foreign, too distant, so when I saw the name Matthew, something familiar about it made me start there. I will be honest; I skimmed most of it. The names were hard to pronounce. The genealogies bored me.

I didn't feel anything.

Until I reached chapter 14.

Jesus walking on water.

Peter stepping out of the boat.

Jesus saying, "Come."

That word broke me.

I fell to my knees and sobbed uncontrollably. Because suddenly, I remembered a dream from my childhood, one that had terrified me. I was six or seven years old. Already abused. Already afraid of men. In the dream, there was a man dressed in white standing in a boat. He stretched his hand toward me and asked me to come to him.

I looked around, only water. No land. Nowhere to run.

The dream had frightened me as a child. But reading that passage as an adult awakened something in me. I realized God had been reaching for me long before I knew how to reach back. Even when I was afraid. Even when I misunderstood Him. Even when I blamed Him. I wept, not out of fear, but remorse. I apologized for cursing Him. For accusing Him. For believing He had abandoned me. I begged for forgiveness without knowing the language for repentance.

I did not know what "born again" meant, at least not the Biblical meaning. I did not know what an altar call was.

I just knew something in me had died, and something new had begun.

For the first time in my life, I felt peace that did not come with strings attached. God was not angry. He was not threatening me. He was not demanding payment.

He showed me grace.

That night, I slept deeply—for the first time in a long time.

A few nights later, everything shifted again.

I fell asleep with the Bible in my hands. And sometime between sleep and wakefulness, I felt someone grab my ankles and pull me off the bed. I felt pressure on my chest, my airway cut off. The room was dark except for a thin crack of light through the blinds.

I could not scream.

I could barely speak.

But I managed to whisper, "Our Father who art in Heaven…"

And instantly, it stopped.

At first, I thought it was a nightmare. Until I saw the redness on my back from the carpet. I knew then it wasn't just a dream. It was spiritual, and it was real.

When I told my friend from the bar, he explained it as spiritual warfare. I had been deeply involved in a satanic cult, and darkness does not release its grip quietly. He told me I needed Scripture, not fear, to stand firm. He directed me to Ephesians 6. I spent six months reading the Bible on my own before ever stepping into a church. Not because I was avoiding church, but because I was learning something new:

God did not need a mediator to reach me.

Not a padrino.

Not a pastor.

Not an institution.

Just me. And Him.

That's when I understood something that would shape the rest of my journey:

God came for me when I stopped chasing Him.

Jesus did not come to bind me with religion.

He came to set me free.

And this was only the beginning.

CHAPTER FIVE:

WHEN FREEDOM STARTED TO FEEL FAMILIAR, AND FEAR RETURNED

After meeting God the way I did, it felt natural to want community. I wanted to be around people who believed. People who loved Jesus. People who understood what had happened to me.

So, I visited churches.

The first one scared me.

The chanting.

People falling over.

Claims of healing power moving through the room.

It felt too close to Santeria, different language, same atmosphere. I left unsettled.

The next church felt nothing like what I remembered from childhood. Instead of quiet reverence, I walked into what felt like a rock concert. Lyrics splashed across giant screens. The music was powerful. The pastor was encouraging. And for the first time, church felt, approachable.

I was welcomed.

Included.

Invited.

I poured myself into the church the way I had poured myself into everything else in my life, with devotion, intensity, and a sincere desire to belong. I attended services, joined groups, volunteered, studied Scripture. I wanted to be obedient. I wanted to grow. I wanted to do this right. I did not realize at the time how familiar that pattern was. I had always believed that belonging came through performance. Through showing up. Through proving worth. Through being useful. And the church, at first, rewarded that instinct.

I felt seen. Valued. Needed.

I joined everything. Small groups. Activities. Even a mission trip to Albania. I wanted connection. I wanted to belong. But there were things I could not name at first, only feel. Every service ended with an altar call: Invite Jesus into your heart.

That language never sat right with me.

Jesus had come to me.

I hadn't summoned Him.

My encounter was organic, not scripted.

Still, I stayed.

There was pressure to tithe, subtle, but constant. I gave out of guilt, convinced obedience meant proving myself to God. Then one Christmas, I received a personal card from the pastor and his wife, an invitation to their home that others did not get. I proudly displayed it, until a friend pointed out, she had never received one in all her years there.

That is when I first realized: My generosity had bought me proximity. It was my first sour note. Later, after prayer and what I believed was the Holy Spirit's guidance, I moved back to New Jersey and attended a much smaller church, Church of the Nazarene. This one was fire-and-brimstone. Scripture-heavy. Disciple-focused.

I felt spiritually illiterate.

So I studied harder. Learned more. Absorbed everything. But instead of clarity, I ended up with more questions than answers. Eventually, I found myself under the Calvary Chapel umbrella and enrolled in Bible institute. Hermeneutics. Apologetics. Theology. I learned the language. I learned how to defend Scripture.

I also learned something else:

Serving was equated with obedience. So, I served. Until I was neglecting my children. When I questioned it, Scripture was used to correct me. Family is whoever does the will of God. (Matthew 12:48–50) I went home and used Scripture on my own kids, trying to force them into church. I felt like a failure. I could explain theology to strangers but could not lead my own children to Christ. My children were not part of my church life. They were old enough to choose, and they chose not to come. I told myself it was okay, that they had their own journeys. But inside, I felt like a failure.

I prayed harder.

Joined more groups.

Tried more formulas.

Nothing worked.

I threw myself deeper into church life. Service became my language of devotion. I filled my schedule with ministries, meetings, studies. I wanted to be obedient. I wanted to be faithful. I wanted to prove that I was "doing it right." But something else was happening quietly.

I was losing myself again.

When I first read the Bible alone, it felt like a love story. Mercy. Grace. God's heart. But now — armed with teaching — it felt condemning. Unlivable. Every question had a rehearsed answer.

Why Deborah, but not women pastors?

Why Paul over lived experience?

Why does the Spirit feel sidelined?

The answer was always the same: The Bible is the final authority. But deep in my spirit, something resisted. The Holy Spirit was the teacher. God was alive, not confined to a system or a book.

Yet I was afraid to say it aloud. I began noticing how pastors were elevated. How Scripture was wielded like a weapon. How faith became robotic, verse for every thought, answer for every doubt. Organic relationship was replaced with performance.

Then came my first "Christian" relationship.

He looked right. Served in ministry. Usher. Motorcycle men's group. I had been searching for love for so long that when it arrived wrapped in Scripture, I did not question it. God was finally blessing me, finally giving me something good after so much loss. What I did not recognize was that I was repeating a familiar pattern: confusing spiritual authority with emotional safety.

But behind closed doors, it was darkness disguised as light. Our relationship was a secret and it didn't have a label. He convinced me no one had to know about us. We had crossed lines. I told him how I felt guilt and shame but he dismiss my feelings. We were fornicating and my nerves were always on edge. I felt that in order to stay with him, I had to perform. A pattern that was so familiar to me. When I suggested pastoral counsel, he refused. He even convinced me that I was a sex addict. I believed him and attended a sex addicts anonymous meeting (SAA).

I didn't belong in SAA. Everything that was being discussed there was nothing I related to. No disrespect to the organization because there are people that are being set free through it. But I was not compulsive. I did not need to have sex and my mind was not consumed with sexual desires. In fact, prior to meeting this man I had been celibate. I started to think he had the issue and projected it unto me. I consistently had a stir in my spirit that something was off. It gave me restless nights. Our conversations were always early mornings, sometimes in the afternoon but never in the evenings. It was a pattern that left me uneasy. But I convinced myself that because he had more years in the faith than I did, he was speaking truth. This turbulent relationship lasted over a year.

Until everything surfaced.

A hidden long-term relationship.

Secret hookups.

Deception.

When I finally spoke up, the church did respond. They removed him from leadership. He was excommunicated.

And for a moment, I felt protected. But then something subtle happened. He was allowed to continue attending the Bible institute, the very place I was attending, the place that was meant to be safe. The reason given was practical. Procedural. Financial. The institution needed tuition, and he was paying it. I was told to trust leadership. To focus on healing. To move forward.

But something inside me cracked.

I had done everything right. I had come forward. I had spoken truth. And yet the message was clear: my safety mattered… but not enough to disrupt the system.

I did not feel angry at first.

I felt small.

I felt expendable.

I began to understand that institutions, even well-meaning ones, often protect structure before people. And that realization hurt more than the original offense.

Still, I stayed.

I told myself this was what faith looked like. Perseverance. Submission. Endurance.

I tried to push down the discomfort and trust that God was working through it.

All I wanted was what I had at the beginning. God. Real. Present. Nearby. I used to close my eyes and envision myself wrapped in a beam of radiant light that kept me safe. It was where I found peace. I could sit at the shoreline and feel His presence all around me. I wanted to feel that once again. A place where I did not need doctrine, rules, or rituals. God is a Person that did not condemn me. What I experienced with God was genuine love.

I changed church four more times before finally stepping away from the institutional church. The fear was loud.

Do not forsake the assembly.

You're deceived.

You're rebellious.

But something else happened too.

Peace returned.

I could hear God again.

I could discern truth without fear.

I could listen without swallowing everything whole.

I did not leave Jesus.

I left the systems that told me fear was faith, guilt was growth, and shame was obedience.

And for the first time in a long time...

Freedom did not feel dangerous anymore. It felt familiar.

CHAPTER SIX:

UNLEARNING FEAR TO RECLAIM FAITH

At first, deconstruction did not feel like freedom. It felt like guilt. I felt lonely, not because God was distant, but because I was afraid to speak openly. I feared judgment from fellow believers. I had spent my entire life overcoming rejection, and I was not willing to invite it to back in through faith.

So, I stayed quiet.

And in that quiet, something unexpected happened: I finally had to face myself. I realized I had hidden behind the Christian banner of service. I stayed busy, involved, committed, praised, but I had not actually taken up my cross the way Jesus described it. Not in my life. For me, taking up my cross was not doing more. It was looking inward.

Why did I still feel like I wasn't enough?

Why did I still crave validation?

Why did approval still matter so much to me?

I had never addressed those questions. I masked them with activity. And I began to wonder, if I had done this, how many other Christians were doing the same? How many of us were hiding in service instead of being transformed in the quiet?

I could not be the only one.

So, I stopped performing and started praying.

I asked God to let me see myself the way He sees me.

And He answered.

Not with condemnation.

Not with correction.

But with identity.

I began to see myself as His daughter. An heir of His kingdom. Someone with direct access to His presence, no mediator needed. And something broke open. I began to love myself, not in pride, but in truth. That love compelled me to sit with each of my children and confess my imperfections. I was not the perfect mother, but I loved them the only way I knew how at the time. I asked for their forgiveness.

Nothing was forced.

Nothing was scripted.

And it freed me.

I began dating myself. Caring for my body. Traveling. Building a healthy life. For the first time, I embraced my singleness, not as lack, but as wholeness. I realized that while I would love a partner, I did not need one to be complete.

God was enough.

His grace truly was sufficient.

I returned to Scripture, not to master it, but to know Him. Not as law, but as Person. The Bible regained its beauty when I stopped using it as a measuring stick and started reading it with spiritual eyes.

The church had always called it the final authority, but it had been taught to me as a rulebook, not a relationship. And rules without relationship never transform. What transformed me was discovering

God's patience. It took thirteen years to come full circle back to that early intimacy, what people call the "honeymoon phase." The difference now is that I know I never have to leave it again.

God is with me in my questions. He is not threatened by my doubts or failures. He does not withdraw His love when I think deeply.

Fear has slowly been replaced with grounded faith.

I read Scripture for pleasure now. When something stirs me, I sit with it. I pray. I wait. And the Holy Spirit teaches, through a stranger, a verse, a message, a quiet knowing.

He always answers.

There is a peace that covers me now, one that brings confidence without arrogance and conviction without fear. That is when I realized something important. The "falling away" is not people leaving God. It is people leaving doctrine that replaced Him. Yes, some walk away from faith entirely. They never believed. But many of us are not leaving God at all. We're leaving institutions that confused control for holiness and fear for faith.

And God never leaves us alone.

He has placed people in my life who believe the same way I do. Who love deeply. Who think freely. Who walk humbly.

My faith today is simple.

Prayer.

Worship.

Gratitude.

Listening.

Knowing God is love and asking daily that His love flow through me to others. I have more grace now. More empathy. Less judgment. And I weep for my brothers and sisters still bound by religious fear, because I remember how critical I became when I was in chains. I see now why so many believers are harsh. They are shackled and do not even know it.

So, I pray for the church, not against it.

That the chains would fall.

That fear would lose its voice.

That love would lead again.

Deconstruction did not destroy my faith.

It delivered it.

CHAPTER SEVEN:

FEARLESS FAITH: LEAVING WITHOUT LEAVING GOD

Fear had been my companion for most of my life. Not the loud, dramatic kind, but the quiet, constant kind that shaped my decisions from the inside out. The kind that whispered caution into every choice and disguised itself as wisdom. I learned early that fear could keep me safe or at least make me feel like I had some control. For a long time, faith meant certainty. That trusting God meant never doubting, never stumbling, never questioning. I thought faith was something to be performed correctly, a set of behaviors and beliefs that, if followed precisely, would keep me protected from pain and failure.

But fear was always underneath it.

Fear of getting it wrong.

Fear of disappointing God.

Fear of falling away.

Fear of being exposed as not "holy enough."

Even my obedience was often fear-driven.

I served because I did not want to disappoint.

I prayed because I was afraid not to.

I stayed quiet because I feared rejection.

And I called it faith. It was not until I stepped away from the noise, away from expectations and performance, that I noticed something unsettling and beautiful at the same time: God did not withdraw from me. I expected distance. I expected silence. I expected consequences. Instead, I found presence. In the stillness, I began to realize that my failures had never disqualified me from God's love. My mistakes had not pushed Him away. My doubts had not offended Him. My questions had not scared Him off.

If anything, my weakness drew Him closer.

That realization undone me.

For so long, I believed that falling meant losing Him. That struggle meant I was failing spiritually. But I began to see that my failures were not evidence of separation, they were invitations into deeper dependence. God was not waiting for me to get it right. He was waiting for me to stop hiding.

I began to understand that conviction and condemnation are not the same. Condemnation crushes. Conviction clarifies. Condemnation demands perfection; conviction invites transformation. And what I experienced was not shame, it was awareness. Gentle, steady awareness. God would bring things to the surface not to accuse me, but to heal me. Not to punish me, but to free me. He showed me patterns that no longer served me, not with anger, but with patience. And when I saw them, I was not forced to change; I was invited. I learned that surrender is not about losing myself. It is about releasing what was never meant to carry me. Every time I stumbled, I discovered that grace met me before I could even reach for it. My falling did not push God away. it brought me closer. Each failure became a place of encounter rather than exile.

This was new.

I had always believed growth meant striving harder. Now I was learning that true transformation comes through surrender, not self-effort.

God was not trying to fix me. He was revealing me, to myself.

And as He did, I began to see how fear had governed so many of my choices. Fear of abandonment. Fear of inadequacy. Fear of being unlovable.

But love, real love, does not run through fear.

Love stays.

Love speaks gently.

Love waits without withdrawing.

And that kind of love began to rewire me from the inside out. I realized that faith was never meant to be fearless in the sense of never trembling. It was meant to be fearless in trust, trusting that even when I stumble, I am held.

Even when I fall, I am not cast out.

Even when I fail, I am still His.

That truth did not make me careless. It made me courageous. Because when you know you are loved beyond performance, you stop running. You stop hiding. You stop pretending.

You begin to live honestly.

And in that honesty, I found something I had searched for my entire life:

Peace.

I started to notice something gentle happening inside me. A softening. A loosening. A quiet trust growing where fear once ruled. I did not need to strive for God's approval; I already had His attention. And that is the part we forget. That faith is not about climbing toward God. It is about realizing He never stepped away.

If you are reading this and something in you feels tender, unsettled, or strangely seen, pause there. Not to fix it. Not to analyze it. Just to notice it. Sometimes the most sacred moments begin not with certainty, but with the courage to stay present with what is stirring inside.

Faith, I am learning, is not the absence of doubt.

It is the willingness to stay open when certainty falls away.

In that openness, something begins to breathe again.

And that is what fearless faith truly is, not the absence of fear, but the willingness to stay present when fear rises. To remain open instead of armoring up. To trust that even in uncertainty, even in weakness, I am not abandoned. I am being held. Slowly, I am learning that faith is not something I have to prove or perform. It is something I return to, again, as I learn to rest in a love that does not recoil when I fall, but draws nearer.

CHAPTER EIGHT:

THE LIES THAT FELL AWAY

I did not recognize the bondage until I stepped outside it.

Inside the church walls, fear had become normal. Fear of hell. Fear of deception. Fear of disappointing leaders. Fear that if my children did not believe exactly the way we were taught, I had failed God. I did not call it bondage then; I called it faithfulness.

Looking back, I see how subtly fear dressed itself as obedience.

I trusted leaders as if their words were God's own voice. And to be fair, some of their counsel was good. But when I prepared to move back to Florida during the pandemic, my mother gone, my season in New Jersey complete, I approached the pastors for prayer and wisdom.

Instead of encouragement, the first question came sharp:

"How do you know that's God's will?"

A seed of doubt planted itself deep. Not intentionally, perhaps, but that's how spiritual control works, quiet, subtle influence. Like Peter being persuaded one moment by revelation and the next by Satan's whisper (Matthew 16:23). I moved anyway. And life shattered. The house was delayed, the commute brutal, depression suffocating. For two years I questioned every decision, tormented by that lingering doubt: Was this God's will? When the heaviness finally broke, it was not through a sermon, it was through surrender.

Enough, I whispered.

And in His gentleness, God reminded me to be grateful in every circumstance. Gratitude softened the edges of disappointment. Peace found cracks and seeped through them. Doors opened, new job, shorter commute, more time to breathe.

But freedom did not mean perfection.

Dating exposed another layer of shame.

Purity culture had trained me to measure myself by failure. To confess sexual sin felt unthinkable, Christians rarely admit those wounds. Shame silenced us. Yet the silence breeds bondage. In stepping away from the institution, I began wrestling with Scripture on my own again, not to justify sin, but to understand covenant. Marriage was not a license; it was self-sacrificial love bound in purpose. That revelation exposed how deeply my childhood trauma warped intimacy. I chased connection through bodies because I did not know how to love myself. Now freedom looks like restraint, not fear-based abstinence, but desire transformed into honor. A willingness to wait, not because the church says so, but because I want covenant, not contracts. And if it never comes, God is enough.

Isolation stripped me bare.

Without programs, pastors, or tradition to hide behind, I had to face myself, my insecurities, my longing for validation, my dependency on spiritual authority. I realized many Christians wear service like armor, numbing their wounds with ministry. I had done the same.

In freedom, the Holy Spirit exposed lies:
that questioning is rebellion
that holiness equals attendance and service
that pastors speak for God
that worth is earned by obedience
that marriage makes you complete
that leaving church means leaving God
Lie by lie, shackles dissolved.

I never told anyone I left the institutional church. The fear was internal fear of being labeled deceived, rebellious, or backslidden. Hebrews 10:25 echoed in my mind like a warning siren. Yet Jesus came to set captives free, not move captivity inside a sanctuary. The narrow road is not paved with religious certainty, it is paved with humility, trust, and surrender. Legalism kept me striving. Freedom brought me face-to-face with grace. And in that place, the throne of grace, I became undone. Not shamed. Not condemned. Seen. Known. Loved.

God did not ask me to be perfect. He asked me to walk with Him, the Perfect One. If you feel that ache, that quiet confusion you cannot articulate, that fear of speaking your doubt aloud, call out to God. He is not threatened by your questions. Shame and guilt are not His tools. His voice is gentle, patient, firm with love. True worship is intimacy with Him, not performance for men.

Freedom isn't rebellion.

It's returning to the One who never left.

CHAPTER NINE:

BECOMING WITHOUT APOLOGY

When the layers of religious pressure fell away, I was surprised by what surfaced.

I had hidden my value in serving.

Without the structure of church and constant activity, I found myself face-to-face with old companions I thought I had buried long ago: feeling unlovable, insecure, not enough. The fear of rejection resurfaced, and before I realized it, I was seeking validation again, this time through dating. Online dating became a mirror I did not ask for.

I was clear about what I wanted: a God-fearing man. But what I encountered instead was rejection dressed in new forms—ghosting, catfishing, silence. Over and over, I felt like the exception to the promise that "there's someone for everyone."

People meant well. They always do.

It will happen when you least expect it.

Work on yourself.

Become the woman a high-value man wants. None of it helped. It only fed the lie that I was still lacking something.

So, I cried out to God.

Why am I still single? Did You not say You'd give me the desires of my heart?

And even as I prayed those words, I realized something uncomfortable, I was treating God like a genie, not my Creator. Guilt followed. The feeling of worthlessness intensified. Then God answered me, but not the way I expected. He used a woman I barely knew. She asked me simple questions that pierced straight through my defenses.

Don't you have a career that sustains you?

Yes.

Don't you own your home?

Yes.

Don't you provide for yourself?

Yes.

Then she said something that settled deep in my soul: You are the daughter of the King of Kings. You do not need to beg for a man's attention. A man needs to find you. That was the moment everything shifted. God had already been confirming me, through provision, protection, and care in every detail of my life. He was not withholding love; He was guarding it. If He is my protector, why would He allow just anyone to sweep me off my feet?

I deleted the dating apps.

Not in bitterness.

In peace.

Prayer and worship became my anchors. And yes, if I am honest, the spirit of insecurity still tries to whisper lies. But now I answer it with truth that lives in my heart, not just on a page. I am wonderfully made. I do not have to fear being alone, I matter deeply to God. Even if others reject me, the Lord holds me close. These truths rise without effort now. This is how the

Holy Spirit teaches me, by reminding me who I am when I forget.

I identify with Christ in rejection.

He knows that pain.

He bore it fully.

And He rose again.

So, when rejection comes, I get back up. I stand on the Rock of my salvation. And strangely enough, that gives me comfort. This season redirected me to care for myself, my body, my mind, my rest. I think about God throughout the day. Not perfectly, but intentionally. And I have noticed something others have noticed too:

I'm lighter.

I glow.

I'm genuinely happy.

I haven't arrived.

I'm becoming.

I know that if God has been faithful to reveal the wrong ones so clearly, He will be faithful to reveal the right one if that is His plan. Not a perfect man. Only God is perfect. But someone who adds value, not drains it. Someone aligned with purpose. And if that never comes, God is still enough. What I would tell anyone in this place, this in-between of longing and healing is simple:

While you are becoming…

just be.

Don't look back.
Don't rush forward.
Be present.
God is here.

CHAPTER TEN:

THE CHURCH JESUS IMAGINED

Leaving the institutional church did not mean I stopped longing for community. It meant I stopped accepting substitutes. For a long time, church was something you attended. A building. A service. A structure you had to fit into or be left out. And when I could not find my place, I assumed the problem was me. But what if it was not? What if my hunger was not for church at all, but for connection? Jesus never invited people into a system. He invited them into relationship. When He spoke of the church, He was not describing a building, a hierarchy, or a weekly event.

He spoke of the called-out ones, people awakened, gathered by love, not controlled by fear. Community was never meant to be forced. Belonging was never meant to be earned. And yet, somewhere along the way, community became conditional. Attendance replaced intimacy. Agreement replaced unity. And love slowly became dependent on compliance. I did not stop believing in community, I started redefining it. Real community began to find me when I stopped searching for it inside walls. God placed people in my life organically, conversations without agendas, friendships without pressure, believers who loved Jesus deeply without needing to police one another's faith.

There were no titles.

No stages.

No tithing records.

No performance.

Just people.

The early followers of Jesus did not gather because they were told to. They gathered because they were transformed. Their unity was not manufactured, it was the natural overflow of shared life, shared meals, shared suffering, shared hope.

That kind of community does not need managing.

It needs nurturing.

Jesus was harshest with religious leaders not because they loved God too much, but because they placed burdens on people God never asked them to carry. They confused holiness with control. Obedience with fear. Authority with power.

And history shows us how quickly that pattern returned, how easily freedom was institutionalized, how fast living faith became doctrine to defend rather than love to embody.

What Jesus called church was never meant to imprison souls.

It was meant to set them free.

Free people do not need constant monitoring.

Free people do not need fear to stay faithful.

Free people gather because love draws them, not because guilt drives them.

This is the church Jesus imagined:

a living body, not an organization.

a family, not a hierarchy.

a movement of love, not a machine of rules.

I did not leave the church because I stopped believing.

I left because I started believing Jesus meant what He said.

And when I let go of the version of church shaped by power, performance, and fear, I discovered that God never intended for me to walk alone.

He intended for me to walk free.

CHAPTER ELEVEN:

FAITH WITHOUT FEAR

For a long time, fear was the engine of my faith.

Fear of hell.

Fear of being deceived.

Fear of disappointing God.

Fear of asking the wrong questions.

Fear kept me obedient, but it never made me free.

When fear is the motivator, faith becomes fragile. You cling tightly, not because you trust God, but because you're afraid of losing Him. And slowly, obedience turns into anxiety disguised as devotion.

I didn't realize how much fear had shaped my faith until it was gone.

When I stepped away from institutional religion, I was told, directly or indirectly, that fear was necessary. That without structure, accountability, and warnings, faith would collapse. That grace without guardrails was dangerous.

But something unexpected happened.

I did not drift away from God.

I leaned into Him.

Without fear pressing me forward, I discovered trust pulling me closer. I prayed more honestly. I listened more deeply. I stopped performing and started resting.

Fear-based faith asks, what happens if I get this wrong?

Love-based faith asks, who is God, really?

And when I began asking that question, everything changed.

I realized fear had trained me to focus on sin more than transformation. On behavior more than the heart. On avoiding punishment rather than pursuing intimacy.

But fear never produces holiness.

Love does.

When love leads, obedience follows, not because it is demanded, but because it's desired. Conviction becomes gentle, not crushing. Correction becomes relational, not condemning.

Fear kept me compliant.

Love made me willing.

I'm not fearless because I am above failure. I am fearless because I trust God's character. I trust that He is patient. That He corrects without humiliating. That He draws rather than drives.

Faith without fear does not make sin appealing, it makes it unnecessary.

When you know you are loved, you stop chasing substitutes. When you trust God's heart, you stop hiding your questions. When shame dissolves, growth begins.

The church taught me to fear getting it wrong.

God taught me to trust Him even when I do not understand.

That is the difference.

Fear says, Stay in line.

Love says, Walk with Me.

And I have learned that walking with God, without fear, has made my faith stronger, not weaker. Deeper, not looser. More honest, not less obedient.

Fear shrinks faith.

Love expands it.

This is faith without fear.

CHAPTER TWELVE:

COMMUNITY WITHOUT CONDITIONS

Leaving the institutional church did not mean I stopped valuing community.

In fact, I missed it.

There are things the church building does well: gatherings, shared worship, prayer nights, meals, celebrations, moments of unity that remind us we are not alone. God designed us for connection. We are relational by nature, and community is not optional for a healthy soul. What I began to grieve was not the gathering itself, but the conditions attached to it.

Over time, I noticed that belonging often came with invisible requirements. Attendance. Agreement. Appearance. Participation in the main service became the gateway to deeper connection. If you were not fully "plugged in," access to community quietly faded. Many people do not leave church because they do not love God.

They leave because they feel unseen.

And many who stay are hiding.

They sit in pews week after week carrying shame, afraid of being discovered. Afraid of asking the wrong questions. Afraid their moral failures will cost them belonging. Afraid that honesty will lead to exclusion rather than healing.

That kind of fear does not produce transformation.

It produces performance.

I am not against people gathering in church buildings. Some thrive there, and that is good. God meets people where they are. He does not force everyone into the same expression of faith. But buildings were never meant to be the gatekeepers of community. The church was always meant to be people, living, breathing, imperfect people, gathered by love, not regulated by fear. The earliest believers met in homes, around tables, in shared life. Their unity was organic. Their connection relational.

The tragedy is not the building.

The tragedy is hiding inside it.

Community should be a place where wounds are tended, not concealed. Where questions are welcomed, not silenced. Where growth is nurtured through grace, not pressure. When community becomes conditional, it stops being safe.

The good news is that God does not abandon us when we step outside the structure. He continues to place people in our lives, sometimes fewer, sometimes quieter, but often deeper. Relationships without agendas. Fellowship without hierarchy. Faith without fear.

I have learned that church does not disappear when you leave a building. It reappears wherever love is practiced, truth is honored, and God is welcomed into the center of ordinary life.

Some are called to stay within church walls and help reshape the culture from the inside. Others are called to step outside and rediscover faith without performance. Neither path is superior.

What matters is freedom.

Community without conditions.

Belonging without fear.

Faith that breathes.

This is the church I believe God intended from the beginning.

CHAPTER THIRTEEN:

THE NARROW ROAD OF FREEDOM

The narrow road is not narrow because it is exclusive. It is narrow because it is honest. When I stepped away from the institutional church, I did not expect the quiet condemnation that followed. Most of it was unspoken concern masked as caution, questions framed as care. I know now it was not intentional. It was indoctrination. A system that teaches people to equate leaving the structure with leaving God.

Still, it hurt.

I had spent years trying to belong. Years proving my devotion through service, attendance, obedience. And when I chose to follow God where He was leading me, outside the familiar, I was met with suspicion instead of trust.

Some assumed I was deceived.

Others assumed I was rebellious.

A few believed I was in danger.

Very few asked if I was free.

This is the cost of the narrow road. It often feels lonely, not because God is absent, but because approval is no longer sourced from people. The irony is that the loudest warnings came from those who believed they were protecting me. They were not trying to harm me. They were repeating what they had been taught: Stay inside the walls. Safety lives there.

But safety was not where God met me.

Freedom was.

The narrow road stripped me of borrowed certainty and returned me to something far more solid—God's presence. Away from constant noise and competing voices, I began to hear Him clearly again. Not through fear. Not through pressure. But through peace. His voice became familiar. Gentle. Consistent.

And that changed everything. I learned that God's approval carries a different weight. It doesn't fluctuate with attendance or agreement. It does not require performance. It rests on relationship.

When I stopped chasing the approval of others, I found the courage to walk where God was leading, even when few understood.

Yes, the narrow road can feel lonely. But it is never empty.

God walks it with you.

And when His voice becomes clearer than the opinions around you, you realize something profound: approval from God is not earned, it is given. And it is enough.

This is why I stay on the narrow road.

Not because it is easy.

Not because it is admired.

But because here. I can hear Him.

CHAPTER FOURTEEN:

THE WORD AND THE LIVING GOD

I want to be clear about something. I love the Bible. I read it every day, not out of obligation, but desire. Scripture has comforted me, corrected me, and drawn me closer to God in ways that feel personal and alive. The Holy Spirit continually speaks to me through it, often illuminating exactly what I need in each season. The Bible has deep value. But it is not meant to be worshipped. Scripture was never intended to replace God. It was written to reveal His character, His heart, and his redemptive work in humanity. It points us to Him—it does not confine Him.

God is living.

He speaks. He leads. He teaches. And while Scripture is one of the primary ways He communicates with us, He is not limited to ink and pages. If He were, there would be no need for the Holy Spirit. This realization did not diminish my reverence for the Bible, it deepened it. I stopped reading Scripture defensively, as something I needed to master or prove, and began reading it relationally, as a testimony that invites encounter. When I did, the words came alive in a way they never had before.

I also began to understand why there are so many Christian denominations.

It is not because God is divided.

It is because interpretation is human.

Culture, history, language, and experience shape how people understand Scripture. That doesn't make believers insincere or unfaithful. It makes them human, seeking an infinite God through finite lenses.

The problem does not arise when people read the Bible differently.

It arises when we claim our interpretation is God. I no longer fear questions. I welcome them.

Questions do not threaten truth. They refine it. Jesus promised the Holy Spirit would guide us into all truth. Scripture affirms this, not as competition, but as harmony. The Word and the Spirit were never meant to be separated.

I don't follow a book.

I follow God.

And I allow Scripture to continually lead me back to Him. This posture has not weakened my faith. It has anchored it. Faith rooted in relationship produces humility, not arrogance. Curiosity, not fear. Love, not division. The Bible stays a sacred gift; one I treasure deeply. But God Himself stays the source.

And that distinction has made all the difference.

CHAPTER FIFTEEN:

FREEDOM REQUIRES DISCERNMENT

Freedom is not the absence of commitment; it is the presence of love. When I first stepped away from the institutional church, I felt lighter, but I also felt exposed. Without a structure telling me what to think, how to serve, or where to stand, I had to learn how to listen again. Not to voices. Not to expectations. But to God. Freedom demanded discernment.

I discovered quickly that freedom without discernment can become reactionary. It can turn into doing the opposite simply because we can. That is not freedom, it is still being led, just in another direction.

God didn't free me so I could drift. He freed me so I could walk intentionally. Discernment is what keeps freedom from becoming careless. It teaches us to pause, to weigh, to listen. It invites humility. It requires honesty, especially with us.

I had to relearn what obedience looked like outside of fear. Not obedience driven by anxiety or guilt, but obedience born from trust. I had to ask different questions:

Is this drawing me closer to God, or distracting me from Him?

Is this nourishing my spirit, or feeding my insecurity?

Is this rooted in love, or in the need to be seen?

Discernment did not make my life easier.

It made it truer.

I learned that freedom does not excuse moral responsibility, it deepens it. When fear is no longer the motivator, integrity must come from within. Conviction becomes personal. Accountability becomes internal. And grace becomes the atmosphere where growth happens.

I no longer needed someone watching me to live with intention. I needed honesty, with God and with myself.

Discernment also taught me boundaries.

Not everyone has access to my heart.

Not every voice gets weight.

Not every opportunity is an open door.

Freedom helped me recognize that saying no can be an act of faith. That waiting is not passivity. That restraint can be worship. And most importantly, discernment taught me compassion. I stopped measuring others by how closely they aligned with my understanding of faith. I learned to honor people where they are, without needing to fix, correct, or rescue them. God does not need my policing. He invites my participation through love.

Freedom with discernment looks quieter than rebellion.

It looks steadier than certainty.

It looks like walking with God rather than proving Him.

I am still learning.

I still pause.

I still listen

I still adjust.

But I am no longer afraid of getting it wrong.

Because discernment has taught me this: God is more committed to shaping me than I am to be perfecting myself. And He is patient, faithful to guide each step when I am willing to follow. Freedom did not remove responsibility.

It refined it. And in that refinement, I found peace.

CHAPTER SIXTEEN:

THE STRENGTH OF BOUNDARIES

There was a time when I believed boundaries meant I was wounded. That if I needed them, I must still be broken. But I see now that boundaries are not a sign of fragility. They are evidence of healing. For much of my life, I confused endurance with love. I thought that if I could tolerate enough, wait long enough, bend far enough, I would finally be chosen. That belief followed me into relationships, friendships, and even faith. I learned to make myself smaller so others could stay comfortable.

So, when I began to name my needs, when I voiced discomfort or asked for clarity, it startled people. Some responded with empathy. Others responded with defensiveness. One man accused me of "playing the victim" when I expressed concern about emotional distance and lack of intentionality. That accusation stung. Not because it was true, but because it echoed an old wound. It sounded like every moment in my life when my pain was dismissed, minimized, or spiritualized away. It sounded like the familiar voice that told me I was "too much" for wanting to be seen, heard, and valued.

But this time, something was different.

I did not collapse under it. I did not scramble to explain myself or shrink my needs to maintain connection.

Instead, I paused.

And in that pause, I recognized something I had not before: this was not rejection, it was revelation. The man was not malicious. He was not evil. He simply could not meet me in the place I now live. And that realization did not require judgment, only discernment. I had mistaken proximity for intimacy before. I had mistaken attention for intention. This time, I could tell the difference. I saw clearly that I was not asking for too much, I was asking the wrong person.

Boundaries, I have learned, are not about control or punishment. They are about alignment. They reveal who can meet you where you are and who is not.

And that's not an indictment, it is information.

Scripture says, "For we wrestle not against flesh and blood, but against principalities, against powers, against the rulers of the darkness of this world."

(Ephesians 6:12)

That verse used to frighten me. Now it clarifies. Because it reminds me that what I meet in others is not always about them, it is often about what moves through them. The resistance, the dismissal, the inability to show up with presence or intention, those are not things I need to fight or internalize. They are simply places where love cannot yet reach.

And I no longer confuse that with my worth. There was a time when I would have absorbed that moment as proof that I was asking for too much. That I was too emotional. Too intense. Too needy. But that woman no longer lives here. Now, I understand that wanting intentionality is not desperation, it is discernment.

Wanting presence is not neediness, it is self-respect. Wanting consistency is not control, it is clarity.

I no longer chase potential.

I respond to presence.

I no longer plead for effort.

I notice alignment.

And I no longer mistake chemistry for connection. What once would have sent me spiraling now simply shows me the door, and I walk through it with peace. Not because I am hardened, but because I am healed enough to trust myself. Boundaries are not walls to keep people out. They are gates that protect what is sacred.

And I am learning to guard what God has been rebuilding in me.

I don't need to explain my worth anymore.

I don't need to earn interest or prove depth.

I don't need to audition for love.

I belong to myself now.

And from that place of belonging, I can choose freely, without fear, without grasping, without shame.

This is not isolation.

This is discernment.

This is not rejection.

This is reverence.

And this—this is what it looks like to walk in freedom.

CHAPTER SEVENTEEN:

ALONENESS IS NOT LONELINESS

For a long time, I believed aloneness and loneliness were the same thing.

I feared being alone because I did not know how to sit with myself. Silence felt like rejection. Stillness felt like failure. And so, I filled my life with people, activity, service, and noise, anything to keep from hearing the voice inside me that whispered, something is still unhealed. What I did not understand then is that aloneness is not abandonment.

It is invitation.

Loneliness, on the other hand, is something entirely different. Loneliness is an assault on the spirit. It tells lies about our worth. It convinces us we are forgotten, undesirable, or incomplete. Loneliness imprisons us in comparison and desperation, urging us to attach to anyone or anything that promises relief, even if it costs us our peace.

Aloneness does the opposite. Aloneness is where God speaks most clearly, not to shame us, but to reveal us to ourselves. It is where distractions fall away and patterns come into focus. It is where we begin to see why we choose what we choose, why we tolerate what we tolerate, and why we keep repeating cycles that never quite satisfy.

Looking back, I can see that the unhealed version of me ran from aloneness because it exposed too much. I mistook loneliness for connection and companionship for alignment. I wanted someone to walk with me, but I had not yet learned how to stand on my own.

Singleness, I have come to believe, is not a punishment or a waiting room. It is a gift. Not because it guarantees clarity or ease, but because it creates space. Space to heal. Space to hear. Space to let God tend to the places that intimacy alone cannot repair. It is in this space that God begins to reorder our desires, not around fear of being alone, but around purpose.

Even within marriage, this truth remains.

Two people becoming one does not mean losing oneself. It requires two whole people, each anchored, each listening, each secure enough to stand alone before they stand together. Aloneness within marriage preserves intimacy. It allows space to hear God individually, so unity is chosen, not demanded. Scripture reminds us that a man who finds a wife finds a good thing and obtains favor from the Lord. But how often do we pause to ask: Who am I becoming before I am found?

Being a godly wife is not about shrinking, giving to silence, or existing in someone else's shadow. It is not about being barefoot, pregnant, or inferior. That narrative has wounded far too many women and misrepresented the heart of God.

In Genesis, woman is called ezer, a helper. Not a servant. Not a subordinate. The root meaning of ezer is strength. It is the same word used to describe God Himself as our helper. That changes everything. A wife is not meant to diminish herself for marriage. She is meant to bring strength, clarity, wisdom, and vision into it.

When we walk in our strength, we do not cling.

We do not beg.

We do not stay where there is no alignment.

We can walk away without bitterness because we are not leaving out of fear, we are leaving out of truth. This is where vision becomes clearer than companionship.

Purpose leads.

Connection follows.

And this applies not only to romantic relationships, but to friendships, communities, and even spiritual spaces. When we are healed, we stop asking Who will choose me? and begin asking Where am I being led? So, I invite you, gently, to reflect.

Are you avoiding aloneness because it feels uncomfortable? Or are you trapped in loneliness because you've been taught you are incomplete on your own? What might God be trying to show you in the quiet you've been resisting?

You do not need another relationship to prove your worth.

You do not need constant companionship to confirm your value.

You need truth, and the courage to sit with it long enough for it to set you free.

Aloneness is not where you disappear. It is where you are revealed.

And from that place, you do not chase alignment, you recognize it.

That is freedom.

CHAPTER EIGHTEEN:

WHEN REJECTION NO LONGER DEFINES YOU

Discernment begins where aloneness has already done its work, where rejection no longer feels personal, but purposeful. It grows quietly, almost unnoticed, in the spaces where we stop rushing to explain ourselves or prove our worth. When we are no longer desperate to be chosen, we become more attentive to what we are choosing.

Old patterns start to surface, not to shame us, but to be recognized. And in that recognition, something shifts. We begin to sense when something is being forced, when peace is absent, and when our spirit is gently warning us to slow down. Discernment does not demand immediate clarity; it invites presence, patience, and honesty with us.

Discernment is not only something we think, but also something we feel. Before I ever had language for it, my body knew. Tightness in my chest. A heaviness that lingered after conversations. A subtle unrest that showed up not as fear, but as confusion. I used to ignore those signals, telling myself I was overthinking, too sensitive, too guarded. But discernment does not announce itself loudly. It speaks through the body and the spirit long before the mind catches up.

There is a difference between nervousness and warning.

Between anticipation and anxiety.

Between peace that stretches you and pressure that depletes you.

When we are unhealed, we override these cues because we don't want to lose connection. We stay where something feels off because rejection feels worse than discomfort. We convince ourselves that love should be hard, that connection requires endurance, that longing is the same as alignment. But discernment grows as we learn to pause.

I've learned to stop asking, why do they feel distant? And start asking, why do I feel unsettled?

That shift changed everything.

Instead of chasing clarity from people, I began asking God for wisdom. Not answers that would rush me forward, but wisdom that would slow me down. I discovered that God does not withhold guidance until we get it right. He gives it generously, without shaming us for needing it. Sometimes wisdom came as clarity. Other times it came as restraint. And often, it came as peace, or the absence of it.

There were moments when I prayed, not for outcomes, but for honesty. Show me what I am not seeing. Reveal what I am afraid to admit. Help me trust what You are already showing me. And slowly, discernment became less about avoiding mistakes and more about honoring myself, I noticed how certain connections drained me while others grounded me. How some conversations left me anxious and overextended, while others allowed me to breathe. How alignment felt steady, not urgent. How genuine interest did not confuse or diminish me, it clarified me.

This is where freedom quietly takes root.

Not in grand declarations, but in small, repeated choices to listen inward instead of reaching outward for validation. Discernment teaches us that we are lovable because something did not work out. We are not abandoned because someone could not meet us where we stood. And we are not rejected; we are being redirected.

So, I invite you to reflect.

Where does your body tense when you think about certain relationships or decisions?

Where does your spirit feel heavy instead of anchored?

Where have you been overriding wisdom because you feared being alone?

You do not need to force answers.

You do not need to confront everything at once.

You do not need to shame yourself for what you did not know before.

Freedom begins when you allow yourself to see clearly, and trust that what you are sensing matters.

Discernment is not about suspicion. It is about self-respect. And it is one of the most loving gifts God offers us as we learn to walk free. As discernment deepens, it gently teaches us what is worth protecting. We begin to understand that the heart is not something to expose carelessly, nor something to barricade in fear. It is something to be guarded with wisdom because everything we do flows from it. And when we ask God for guidance, not hurriedly, not out of anxiety, but with trust, He meets us there, generously and without reproach. This is where discernment matures into stewardship, and where learning to guard the heart becomes an act of love rather than defense.

CHAPTER NINETEEN:

GUARDING THE HEART WITHOUT BUILDING WALLS

For a long time, I confused guarding my heart with shutting it down.

I thought if I stayed distant enough, detached enough, careful enough, I would never be hurt again. But that kind of protection is not wisdom, its fear dressed up as strength. And fear always asks us to shrink, never to grow.

Guarding the heart is not about isolation. It is about stewardship. I have learned that my heart is not something to hand over recklessly, nor is it something to lock away and pretend it does not long to be seen. It is something sacred, something entrusted to me. And everything I do flows from it. There were seasons when I ignored what my heart was telling me because I did not want to appear difficult, needy, or afraid of being alone. I explained away the tightness in my chest. I dismissed the confusion that lingered after conversations. I overrode discernment with hope, or worse, with chemistry.

But wisdom does not demand certainty. It invites honesty. I have discovered that when I slow down enough to ask God for wisdom, He does not withhold it. He does not mock my questions or shame my hesitation. He meets me in it, generously, patiently, helping me see what I couldn't see before because I was afraid to look.

Sometimes wisdom comes as clarity.

Other times it comes as restraint.

And often, it shows up as peace, or the absence of it.

I now understand that when something feels off, it does not mean I am broken or too guarded. It means my spirit is paying attention. Discernment is quiet. It rarely announces itself. It nudges. It waits. It asks us to listen instead of rush.

Guarding my heart has meant learning to pause before attaching, to see before investing, to pray before explaining things away. Not because I am afraid of love, but because I finally understand my value. This has changed how I relate to people, especially in romantic spaces. I no longer feel the need to prove my worth by being accommodating, available, or endlessly understanding. Love does not require self-abandonment. Connection does not demand silence. And interest should never feel confusing.

I'm learning that wisdom and vulnerability can coexist.

That openness does not mean overexposure.

That guarding the heart does not make me cold, it makes me grounded.

And when rejection comes, because sometimes it still does, it no longer devastates me. It clarifies. It reveals where I was willing to settle and where God was quietly protecting me from doing so. I do not need to harden my heart to survive anymore. I need to honor it.

Because the more I walk in wisdom, the more my heart stays soft, not toward everyone, but toward the right things. Toward truth. Toward peace. Toward love that reflects God's character rather than my old wounds.

Guarding the heart isn't about keeping people out. It is about keeping God close enough to lead.

CHAPTER TWENTY:

BECOMING SAFE TO YOURSELF

There comes a moment in healing when the question is no longer What happened to me?

It becomes Can I trust myself again?

For many of us, especially those who have lived through trauma, abandonment, or repeated disappointment, self-trust is not automatic. It was interrupted early. We learned to doubt our instincts because listening to them did not keep us safe. So we adapted. We learned to read rooms, expect moods, minimize needs, and override our inner voice for the sake of peace.

Over time, that distance from ourselves became familiar.

And familiarity can masquerade as normal.

Becoming safe to yourself is the quiet work of reversing that pattern. It is learning to sit with your own thoughts without judgment. To notice what you feel without at once correcting it. To listen inward without rushing to explain it away.

This kind of safety does not come from control.

It comes from compassion.

I used to believe strength meant pushing through discomfort, ignoring intuition, and staying agreeable. Now I understand that strength often looks like pausing. It looks like saying, something about this does not feel right, even when you cannot fully articulate why.

It looks like honoring your limits without apologizing for them.

Many people fear that listening to themselves will make them selfish, cold, or distant. But the opposite is true. When you are safe with yourself, you stop seeking safety from others in unhealthy ways. You stop attaching to what soothes temporarily but costs you long-term peace.

You no longer abandon yourself to be chosen.

Becoming safe to yourself also means learning how to forgive yourself, not once, but repeatedly. Forgiving yourself for what you did not know. For what you tolerated. For the ways you survived when survival was all you had.

Self-forgiveness is not indulgence.

It is restoration.

It allows you to move forward without dragging shame behind you. It gives you permission to grow without constantly rehearsing your past.

Faith plays a quiet but essential role here. When I began to trust that God was not disappointed in me, I slowly learned how to stop being disappointed in myself. When I stopped viewing God as a critic, I stopped treating myself like one.

The voice that once rushed me, pressured me, or shamed me began to lose authority. In its place grew a steadier voice one that invited discernment, patience, and honesty.

That voice did not rush decisions.

It did not demand certainty.

It did not shame hesitation.

It guided.

And as I learned to listen to it, I noticed something profound: peace became my reference point. If something required me to betray my values, silence my concerns, or override my intuition, it was not alignment, it was familiarity trying to reclaim ground. Safety with yourself means you no longer need chaos to feel alive. You no longer confuse intensity with connection. You no longer chase what costs you your center.

Instead, you move slowly.

You choose carefully.

You listen deeply.

And when you stumble, because you will, you do not collapse into self-condemnation. You course-correct with kindness. You ask for wisdom. You begin again.

This is not perfection.

This is maturity.

Becoming safe to yourself is not a destination. It is a relationship, one that grows stronger the more you honor it. And as that safety deepens, fear loosens its grip.

You stop living defensively.

You stop bracing for disappointment.

You stop preparing for abandonment.

Because you know, no matter what happens, you will not leave yourself behind.

And that changes everything.

For a long time, my story was something to endure quietly, not something to speak aloud. I thought my pain disqualified me, that my failures made my voice less credible, my journey less worthy of being heard. But healing has taught me otherwise.

What nearly broke me became the very place God met me most intimately. Scripture says we overcome by the blood of the Lamb and by the word of our testimony. Not by perfection. Not by having it all figured out. But by truth. I no longer see my testimony as exposure. I see it as evidence. Evidence that God redeems what was meant to destroy. Evidence that nothing is wasted. And evidence that freedom is not an idea to be studied, it is a life to be lived, and a story meant to be shared.

FINAL CHAPTER:

FROM SHACKLES TO FREEDOM

For most of my life, I lived imprisoned long before I ever recognized the bars.

They were not visible. They did not clank when I moved. But they were heavy shackles forged from fear, shame, rejection, and the quiet belief that something was wrong with me. That belief shaped my choices, my relationships, my faith, and even how I understood God.

I searched everywhere for relief.

In achievement.

In relationships.

In spirituality.

In religion.

But nothing loosened the chains because I was looking for freedom everywhere except where it lives.

Freedom did not come when I learned more rules or mastered better behavior. It did not come when I tried harder to be acceptable, obedient, or worthy. Freedom came when I stopped chasing religion and began seeking the living God.

Not a system.

Not a doctrine.

Not a performance.

A presence.

The God I encountered did not bind me tighter, He unbound me. He did not shame me for where I had been or threaten me with what would happen if I failed again. He met me where I was and began doing what only He can do: restoring what fear had stolen, untangling lies I had mistaken for truth and teaching me how to live from love instead of survival.

Freedom, I have learned, is not the absence of struggle. It is the absence of fear-driven living. I am free now, not because I have arrived, but because I am no longer hiding. I am free because my failures no longer exile me from God's presence. They draw me closer. I am free because shame no longer has authority over my identity. I am free because rejection no longer defines my worth.

This freedom is not static. It is alive.

I am still becoming.

Still learning.

Still shedding layers that once protected me but no longer serve me.

I still want a spouse. I still believe in partnership, connection, and shared purpose. But I will not trade my freedom for companionship. I will not abandon myself just to avoid physical aloneness. Loving myself, genuinely loving myself, has taught me that settling is not intimacy, and presence is not the same as alignment.

Spiritually, I am never alone.

God has been faithful to His promise: He has never left me. Not in my doubt. Not in my wandering. Not in my questions. His presence has been my anchor, my refuge, and my freedom.

Freedom, I now understand, is living awake.

It is choosing truth over fear.

Love over shame.

Grace over striving.

And this freedom is not reserved for a few; it is God's desire for all of us.

Jesus said that we would know the truth, and the truth would set us free. He was not offering information; He was offering Himself. And when fear loosens its grip, when shame loses its voice, when love becomes the loudest truth we know, the shackles fall.

Not all at once.

But enough to walk forward.

This is not the end of my story.

It is the place where I finally stand unbound.

And if my journey has done anything at all, I hope it reminds you of this:

You are not broken beyond repair.

You are not disqualified by your past.

You are not alone.

Freedom is possible.

And it begins, not in religion, but in the living God who has been seeking you all along.

A Closing Reflection

If you have reached this point, I want to invite you to pause, not to evaluate yourself, but to breathe. This journey may have stirred memories, questions, or emotions you did not expect. That is not a sign of weakness. It is a sign that something within you is waking up.

You do not need to rush what comes next. Healing does not ask for urgency; it asks for honesty. There may be parts of your story you have avoided, parts you have carried quietly, parts you have judged yourself for far too long. Freedom doesn't come from fixing those parts, it comes from seeing them clearly and refusing to let them define you.

Take a moment to notice what resonated most. Where did your body tense? Where did your heart soften? Those places matter. They are often where truth is already at work, inviting you to release fear, shame, or the belief that you must earn love to be worthy of it.

You are allowed to be in process.

You are allowed to question without abandoning faith.

You are allowed to choose freedom without having every answer.

Whatever your next step looks like, let it come from truth rather than fear, from love rather than obligation. Trust that you are not walking alone, even when the path feels quiet. Freedom has a way of meeting us when we stop running from ourselves and allow light to do what it does best: reveal, restore, and lead us forward.

As you close these pages, I invite you to turn inward, not to judge yourself, but to listen. There is a quiet place within you where truth has always been speaking, even when you did not know how to hear it. Freedom does not begin with religion or striving; it begins when the shackles fall and truth takes root. You were never created to live bound by fear, shame, or the need to earn love. The Spirit who brings life and renewal is already at work within you, leading you from bondage into freedom, repeatedly. This is what it means to be born again: not a moment confined to the past, but a continual awakening into truth. The freedom you are looking for is close to you. It is already unfolding within.

www.ingramcontent.com/pod-product-compliance
Lightning Source LLC
Chambersburg PA
CBHW050952050726
47592CB00007B/2531